Consultants

Ashley Bishop, Ed.D.

Sue Bishop, M.E.D.

Publishing Credits

Dona Herweck Rice, *Editor-in-Chief*

Robin Erickson, *Production Director*

Lee Aucoin, *Creative Director*

Sharon Coan, *Project Manager*

Jamey Acosta, *Editor*

Rachelle Cracchiolo, M.A.Ed., *Publisher*

Image Credits

cover Plcsfive/Shutterstock; p.2 Plcsfive/Shutterstock; p.3 Maksym Gorpenyuk/Shutterstock; p.4 newphotoservice/
Shutterstock; p.5 Gelpi/Shutterstock; p.6 hamurishi/Shutterstock; p.7 Andresr/Shutterstock; p.8 Stephen Coburn/
Shutterstock; p.9 Maxim_Kovalev/Shutterstock; p.10 MTrebbin/Shutterstock; back cover Maksym Gorpenyuk/
Shutterstock

Teacher Created Materials

5301 Oceanus Drive
Huntington Beach, CA 92649-1030
http://www.tcmpub.com

ISBN 978-1-4333-2546-5
© 2012 Teacher Created Materials, Inc.
Printed in China
Nordica.072018.CA21800635

I see a **b**ear.

I see a **bird**.

I see a **butterfly**.

I see a boy.

I see a bike.

I see a **bus**.

I see a boat.

I see a ball.

I see a book.

Glossary

ball   bear   bike

bird   boat   book

boy   bus   butterfly

Sight Words

I   see   a

Activities

- Read the book aloud to your child, pointing to the *b* words as you read them. After reading each page, ask, "What do you see?"

- Go to a park and look for birds. Talk about the way the birds look and sound. Then, have your child draw a picture of the experience and help him or her label the picture with the word *bird*.

- Use describing words that start with the letter *b* to describe the pictures in the book. For example, say to your child, "I see a blue bike," or "I see a big bus." Challenge your child to think of other *b* words and to use them in sentences.

- Have your child look through a magazine to find pictures of things that start with the letter *b*. Have him or her make a collage with the pictures.

- Help your child think of a personally valuable word to represent the letter *b*, such as *boat*.